AM I DEAD?
THIS IS NICE.
FEELS LIKE *HOME*.
IT WON'T LAST.
WHAT DOES *INTESTATE* MEAN?!

HISSSSSSSSSSSSSSSSSSS

MEDIA WANTS THEIR STORY.

AGING ROCK STAR GETS FAT. GOES BALD. PUTS OUT GREATEST HITS ALBUM.

DOESN'T MOVE THE NEEDLE.

'TEEN ANGST JESUS' DEAD AT 27. CONSUMED BY FORTUNE, FAME AND EXCESS.

CELEBRATE HIS LIFE WITH THIS COLLECTIBLE PICTURE BOOK AND VHS TAPE WITH COMMEMORATIVE PIN.

OPERATORS ARE STANDING BY.

I COULD QUIT. BECOME A RECLUSE. DO JUNK ALL DAY. SELL PAINTINGS AND POEMS FOR MONEY.

I MISS LOVE.

I MISS BEING IN LOVE. I MISS *BEING* LOVED. I MISS SHARING THINGS. WE USED TO SHARE EVERYTHING.

I'M BORED SICK JUST THINKING ABOUT IT.

EVERYTHING WAS NEW.

AND IMPORTANT.

AND *PRECIOUS.*

NOW SHE KNOWS WHAT I'M GOING TO SAY BEFORE I SAY IT.

WANNA *FUCK?*

ZZZZZ

EVERYTHING FADES.
KNOCK
SO YOU FILL IN THE HOLES.
GOT ANYTHING?
JUST SOME BOOZE, MAN. SORRY.
GROAN
IT'S REALLY HIM! OH MY GOD! HE'S SOOO HOT!
I TOLD YOU IT WAS HIM! I TOLD YOU!
MY FANS KEEP GETTING YOUNGER.

MINERVA FRONTMAN DEAN DILLON WAS RELEASED FROM A MANCHESTER HOSPITAL THIS MORNING AFTER SUFFERING FROM AN APPARENT OVERDOSE OF SLEEPING MEDICATION.

DILLON'S WIFE, DEBBIE AMORE, STATED THAT THE OVERDOSE HAD BEEN "AN ACCIDENT" AND THAT SHE AND HER HUSBAND WOULD BE RETURNING TO THEIR SEATTLE HOME TO RECUPERATE.

AMORE ALSO STATED THAT THE BAND WOULD BE GOING AHEAD WITH THEIR PLANS TO HEADLINE THIS SUMMER'S GRUNGE-A-PALOOZA TOUR.

MINERVA WAS IN MANCHESTER AS PART OF THE FIRST LEG OF THEIR EUROPEAN TOUR.

THE REMAINDER OF THAT TOUR HAS BEEN CANCELED.

~♥?

~♥!

TIMES
OVERDOSE NO ACCIDENT

ACCIDENTS HAPPEN, IT'S ROCK 'N' ROLL! HE'LL MAKE THAT MONEY BACK AT *GRUNGE-A-PALOOZA* THIS SUMMER..

MAKE SURE YOU BRING THOSE PAPERS OVER FOR HIM TO SIGN. AND LET'S TRIM THE FAT FROM HIS RECORD DEAL. THE NEW TERMS ARE-

HE RETAINS 95 PERCENT WITH THE REMAINING FIVE PERCENT TO BE SPLIT BETWEEN THE TWO OF YOU.

I THINK WE ALL KNOW WHO THE *ENGINE* OF THIS MACHINE IS.

*JESUS,* MAN. TWO AND A HALF PERCENT?

"THE *GOOD* NEWS IS PROFITS FROM TOURING REMAIN AN EQUAL THREE WAY SPLIT."

"IF I WERE YOU I'D BE SURE TO TELL HIM HOW IMPORTANT *GRUNGE-A -PALOOZA* IS TO YOU."

WHY WOULD HE DO THIS?

HE DIDN'T DO THIS.

MERVYNS Recording Session

Producer:
DEAN DILLON

HOW WAS THAT, *DEAN?*

UHHH, DEAN'S NOT HERE.

Meanwhile...

I HATE MYSELF FOR BEING WHAT PEOPLE WANT ME TO BE.

I HATE MYSELF FOR *NOT* BEING WHAT PEOPLE WANT ME TO BE.

KILLING YOURSELF SHOULD BE EASIER.

THERE SHOULD BE A BUTTON YOU CAN PRESS OR A SWITCH YOU CAN THROW.

WHY IS IT SO FUCKING HARD?

THE MOTHER EVICTS THE CHILD FROM THE WARMTH AND PROTECTION OF THE WOMB.

INTO A COLD AND INHOSPITABLE WORLD.

THE CHILD MUST THEN SUFFER THE HARSHNESS OF LIFE ON ITS OWN.

OFTEN, A SENSE OF REJECTION OR DEFECT CAN PERSIST.

DUDE?

DUDE!? YOUR CHICK'S ON THE PHONE. SAYS YOUR KID HAD AN ACCIDENT.

A FUCKING INTERVENTION...
YOU CANCELED THE LAST TOUR. YOU'VE MISSED RECORDING SESSIONS...
YEAH, MAN. AND GRUNGE-A-PALOOZA MEANS A LOT TO US.
WE'RE REALLY WORRIED ABOUT YOU.
YOU'RE ALL LIARS AND HYPOCRITES.
ALL YOU CARE ABOUT IS MONEY.
FIND A NEW GOLDEN GOOSE.
I'M DONE.

WHEN THE PAIN OF LIVING-
KLICK
OUTWEIGHS THE FEAR OF DYING.
CONGRATULATIONS, LEECHES.
YOU JUST TIPPED THE SCALE.
TINK TINK TINK TINK
OH FUCK...

YOU FUCKING COWARD.

DID YOU DROP THE BULLETS DOWN THE VENT ON PURPOSE?

YOU'RE SUCH A DISAPPOINTMENT.

EVERYONE IN THAT ROOM IS DISAPPOINTED.

NOT THAT YOU'VE ABANDONED THEM.

KLIK

CH. 19

THEY'VE COME TO EXPECT THAT.

BUT THAT THE ONLY SOUND FROM THIS ROOM IS SILENCE—

PLINK

AND NOT A GUNSHOT FOLLOWED BY YOUR BRAINS SPILLING OUT ONTO THE FLOOR.

LAX

Spa and Rehabilitation
Center

DO YOU WANT TO GET CLEAN?

NOT REALLY.

THEN *WHY* ARE YOU HERE?

BECAUSE I WANT MY WIFE TO LOVE ME AGAIN.

IT'S NOT GOING TO WORK.

HUH?

"IN ORDER TO BE LOVED YOU HAVE TO BE SOMEONE *WORTHY* OF LOVE. I SUSPECT THE REASON FOR YOUR MARITAL PROBLEMS IS THAT YOU DON'T *THINK* YOU'RE THAT PERSON RIGHT NOW.

*EVERYTHING IN LIFE IS A CHOICE.* YOU CHOOSE TO BE AN ADDICT. YOU CHOOSE TO BE ALONE. YOU CHOOSE TO BE UNHAPPY.

BUT YOU CAN CHOOSE TO BE SOMETHING ELSE. YOU CAN CHOOSE TO BE A GREAT HUSBAND. A GREAT FATHER. A GREAT MUSICIAN.

ALL IT IS *IS* A CHOICE. A CHOICE BETWEEN THE PERSON YOU ARE AND THE PERSON YOU WANT TO BE."

"YOU CAN BE *REMEMBERED* AS A SAD, LONELY ADDICT..."

"OR YOU CAN BE *KNOWN* AS SOMETHING ELSE."

"NOW-"

"WHY ARE YOU *HERE?*"

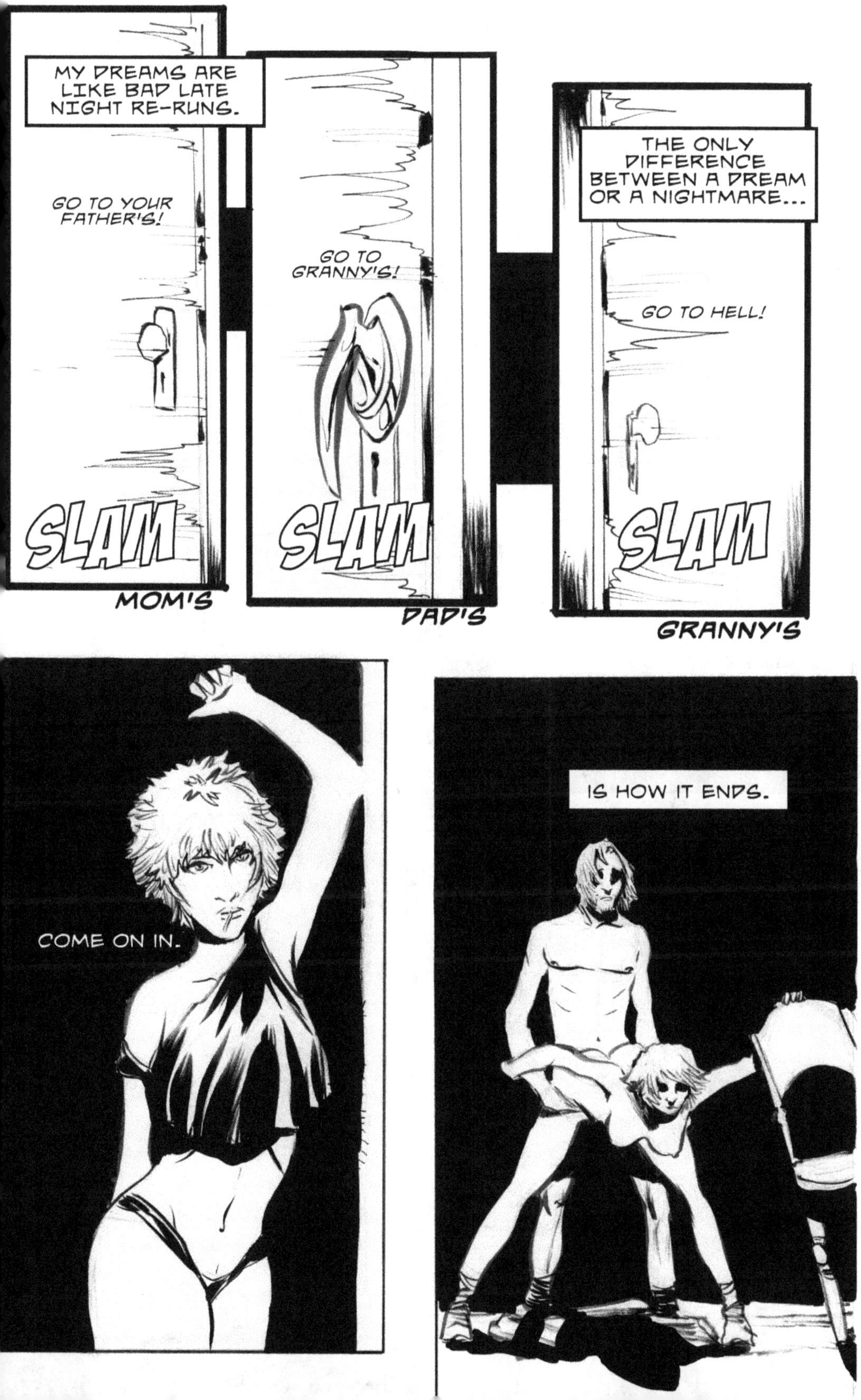
MY DREAMS ARE LIKE BAD LATE NIGHT RE-RUNS.
GO TO YOUR FATHER'S!
SLAM
MOM'S
GO TO GRANNY'S!
SLAM
DAD'S
THE ONLY DIFFERENCE BETWEEN A DREAM OR A NIGHTMARE...
GO TO HELL!
SLAM
GRANNY'S
COME ON IN.
IS HOW IT ENDS.

HI, IT'S ME AGAIN. I'M CALLING TO SEE IF THERE ARE ANY UPDATES ON MY HUSBAND'S PROGRESS?

OH, **WONDERFUL!** PLEASE LET HIM KNOW THAT I CALLED AND THAT I'M PROUD OF HIM AND THAT THINGS ARE GOING **GREAT** OVER HERE.

IT'S FINANCIALLY *IMPERATIVE* THAT HE BE AT HIS BEST IN A FEW WEEKS FOR GRUNGE-A-PALOOZA.

NO WAY! IT'S MR. MUSIC TELEVISION! THEY GOT YOU TOO?

HEY.

HOP THAT FENCE, MAN —WE CAN SCORE IN TWENTY MINUTES. I KNOW A GUY OVER AT THE PALMS HOTEL.

NAH, I'M GOOD.

BED CHECK. EVERYTHING OK?

EVERYTHING IS GREAT.

CH. 13

HOW DO YOU WANT THIS STORY TO END?

SHE'S A VIBRANT WOMAN WHO ENJOYS THE COMPANY OF OTHER VIBRANT PEOPLE.

YOU'RE A JUNKIE WHO ROOTS IN FILTH AND HAS TO BE BABYSAT LEST HE SWALLOW HIS OWN TONGUE.

YOU'RE NOT UNWORTHY OF LOVE. YOU'RE UNLOVABLE. THERE'S A DIFFERENCE.

YOU'RE AN ANTHEM. A T-SHIRT. A POSTER ON A DORM ROOM WALL. AND WITH EACH PASSING DAY THAT FADES.

YOU ARE NOT IMPORTANT. YOUR MYTH IS IMPORTANT. DO YOUR CHILD A FAVOR. LEAVE HER THE MYTH.

THE TV IS RIGHT...

HE BOUGHT A PLANE TICKET TO SEATTLE. I CANCELED HIS CREDIT CARD AND CALLED THE NANNY—

"AND I NARC'D ON HIS DEALER."

LOOK, IF YOU WANNA HOP ON A PLANE, I UNDERSTAND. I'M SURE YOU COULD FIND HIM.

I NEED TO CALL OUR LAWYER TO SEE IF HE'S FILED DIVORCE PAPERS.

WHAT IF HE'S WITH ANOTHER **WOMAN**?

WHAT IF HE **DIVORCES** ME AND CUTS ME OUT OF HIS **WILL**?

THAT CAN'T HAPPEN. THINK OF SOMETHING... **THINK!**

CALL THE PRESS. YOU'RE TAKING ME TO THE HOSPITAL. I'LL FAKE AN OVERDOSE. THAT'LL GET HIS FUCKING **ATTENTION**.

SOO— HOW MUCH DID YOU NEED?

ALL OF IT.

H—HOW MUCH?

ALL OF IT.

MINERVA, INC
124 PATHWAY DR
SEATTLE, WA 98121

$

PAY TO THE
ORDER OF

D.D.

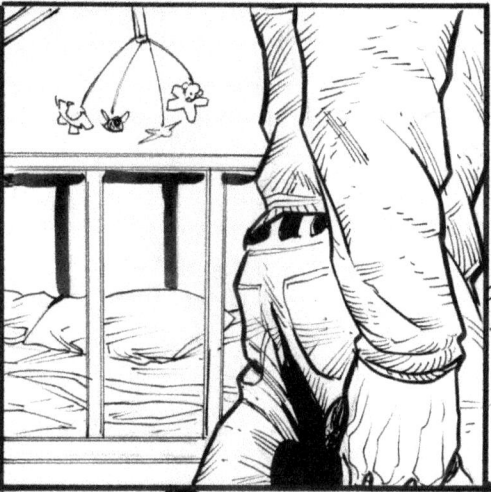

BUT LIFE *ISN'T* A CHOICE.
WHEN YOU COME AND WHEN YOU GO IS UP TO SOMETHING ELSE. *SOMEONE* ELSE.
YOU'RE SHAT OUT NAKED AND AFRAID. TOLD TO OVERCOME YOUR INSTINCTS. OVERCOME YOUR NATURE.
CHOOSE TO BE WHAT *WE* WANT YOU TO BE.
AND WHEN YOU'RE PATHETIC AND BROKEN WE'LL SHOW YOU THE DOOR.
CHOOSE *LIFE?*
LIFE ISN'T A CHOICE. IT'S A RAPE VICTIM WITH STOCKHOLM SYNDROME.
I'LL SHOW MYSELF OUT, THANKS.
YOU CAN'T FIRE ME BECAUSE *I QUIT.*

www.ingramcontent.com/pod-product-compliance
Lightning Source LLC
Chambersburg PA
CBHW060547030426

42337CB00021B/4480